Go

Little book of

Christmas

Words of promise, hope
and celebration

RICHARD DALY

WILLIAM
COLLINS

First published in Great Britain in 2013
by William Collins
An Imprint of HarperCollins*Publishers*
77–85 Fulham Palace Road
London W6 8JB

www.williamcollinsbooks.com

3 5 7 9 10 8 6 4 2

© 2013 Richard Daly

Richard Daly asserts the moral right to be
identified as the author of this work

A catalogue record for this book is
available from the British Library

ISBN 978-0-00-752833-2

Printed and bound in China by
South China Printing Co. Ltd.

Introduction

Christmas is such a joyful time. Somehow it creates an excitement and buzz that extends to all ages. For many this is one of the most wonderful times of the year. While today unfortunately Christmas has become overly commercialised, the real reason for the season will always remain.

Christ is the Saviour of the world. He came to seek and to save; he left his heavenly abode with its perfect surroundings to live with us in our imperfect surroundings. He left the adoration and praise of his angels to receive insult and rejection from his own created. He suffered and died so that we can have life. Why did he do all this?

To save a dying world from the consequences of sin, to give us hope and an eternal future. Christ came because he loves us.

Christmas is really about acknowledging what Christ has done and giving thanks that he came. This King of kings who was born in lowly conditions will one day return so that we can all share in his heavenly riches.

Richard Daly

Glory in the highest

Christ came to live in lowly surroundings
so that one day we can live with him in
heavenly surroundings.

For Further Reflection
Luke 2:12–16

The man for all seasons

Christ is the reason for the season, the truth
for today and hope for tomorrow.

For Further Reflection

John 14:6

Take time to reflect

Christmas ought to be a time of reflection, a
time to contemplate the mystery of why God
became man. The answer is found in love.

For Further Reflection
1 John 4:10

Surprise someone

During this season more people are open
to a spirit of good will and cheer. It's a great
opportunity to do random acts of kindness
without being questioned.

For Further Reflection

Ephesians 4:32

Spend wisely

Resist the overspend on food during
this time and try to spare some cash for
a local charity providing gifts to children;
it will bring a smile.

For Further Reflection
Luke 21:1–4

O come, all ye faithful

'I will honour Christmas in my heart and try to keep it all the year.'

Charles Dickens

For Further Reflection
Hebrews 13:8

Reason for the season

With all the commercialism surrounding the day, do what you can to put Christ back into Christmas. Share the real meaning.

For Further Reflection
John 12:32

Be thankful

Christ came from heaven to earth and gave
us the greatest gift – himself.

For Further Reflection

John 3:16

He'll be back!

As surely as Christ came the first time,
according to his promise we can confidently
look forward to his 'second coming', this time
as King of kings and Lord of lords.

For Further Reflection
John 16:16

Amazing grace

The gift of grace is an active, energising
element that enables you to do what you
cannot do in your own strength.

For Further Reflection
Romans 3:24

Let God deal with it!

God is interested in every detail of your
life. If something is important to you, it's
important to him. Nothing fazes him.

For Further Reflection

Philippians 4:6

Your future's in good hands

The birth of the baby Jesus stands as the
most significant event of all time; it divides
history from BC to AD and gives hope
to an unseen future.

For Further Reflection
Psalm 31:24

Spend time with loved ones

Many view Christmas as a time of spending quality time with the family, but why do we have to wait for Christmas to do that?

For Further Reflection
John 15:13–17

Keep the spirit alive

'Wouldn't life be worth the living
Wouldn't dreams be coming true
If we kept the Christmas spirit
All the whole year through?'

For Further Reflection
Romans 8:35–39

Joyful, joyful

'Joy to the world, the Lord has come.
Let all the earth rejoice!'

For Further Reflection

Psalm 100

Do not fear

'And his name shall be called Emmanuel
(which means "God with us")' ... be assured
that whatever you go through, the very name
of God reminds you that you are not alone.

For Further Reflection
Matthew 1:23

You are sought after

The whole mission of Christ was to 'seek and to save the lost' ... Christ came all the way from heaven just to find you and save you.

For Further Reflection
Luke 19:10

What child is this?

The blessed life which began in Bethlehem
two thousand years ago is one that will give
hope for many centuries to come.

For Further Reflection

Matthew 28:20

Reflect

During this season look back over the past year to remind yourself how God has blessed you ... then take time to give him thanks.

For Further Reflection

Psalm 5:11–12

Live meaningfully

Your greatest gift is your God-given life;
only you can decide how to make
the best of it.

For Further Reflection
Ecclesiastes 9:10

Enjoy today

Your past is behind you, your future is yet
to be revealed, the only thing you have is
the present, and that's why it's a gift ...
seize the moment.

For Further Reflection
Psalm 118:24

Live peaceably

Peace and goodwill are often the sentiments
offered during this season ... but they're yours
to enjoy throughout the year. Christ says,
'Peace I leave with you; my peace I give you.'

For Further Reflection

John 14:27

Discover the meaning
of Advent

To understand the concept of the great
God condescending into human flesh and
living among us, is to truly understand
the plan of salvation.

For Further Reflection
Colossians 1:26–27

Be thankful

In spite of the many benefits God has blessed
us with, how many times do you complain
and moan about little difficulties and trials?
Put your life into perspective; develop
an attitude of gratitude.

For Further Reflection

Colossians 3:15

Pass on the love

During this Advent season as we reflect on
the committed relationship God has toward
us, let us reflect this commitment toward
our own family and loved ones.

For Further Reflection

John 15:12

Yours for the taking

Struggling with disappointments at Christmas? Look under the 'tree of life' – you'll find an inexhaustible supply of gifts from the Prince of Peace waiting to be opened all year round.

For Further Reflection

Revelation 22:2,14

Claim your joy

The angel's proclamation at Christ's birth was 'Fear not ... I bring you good tidings of great joy...' These words still ring true today, more than ever before in your life.

For Further Reflection
Luke 2:10

Worship the Saviour

The wise men sought Jesus not just to bring gifts, but to worship him; the wise are still needed to seek and worship Christ today.

For Further Reflection

Matthew 2:11

You are not alone

If we could condense all the truths about Christmas into just three words they would be, 'God with us.'

For Further Reflection
Matthew 1:23

Born lowly, reigns highly

More astonishing than a baby in a manger,
is the truth that this promised child is the
Omnipotent Creator of the entire universe.

For Further Reflection

John 1:1–6

Heavenward bound

Christ who came also promised to return to take us to his heavenly home. This world is not our home, we're just passing through.

For Further Reflection

Hebrews 11:13

You're highly valued

'It's the thought that counts' is a true saying – likewise, the thoughts God has towards you in sending Christ. He says, 'You are precious in my sight.'

For Further Reflection

Jeremiah 29:11

Give with a willing heart

Christmas is a time to remind us that it is 'more blessed to give than to receive'.

For Further Reflection

Luke 6:38

Choose to be happy

Contentment is simply appreciating the
moment and making the best of your current
situation. It comes by choice rather than
being dictated by circumstances.

For Further Reflection
Philippians 4:11

Get ready for a blast

It took just one angel to announce the good tidings of great joy; it will take ten thousand times ten thousand and ten thousand more to proclaim his triumphant return.

For Further Reflection

Revelation 5:11

Let Christ clean you up

The only gift you can give in return for what
Christ has done for you is a surrendered life,
still plagued with life's troubles and issues.
Christ's appeal is, 'Just come as you are'.

For Further Reflection

Proverbs 23:26

Keep things simple

Last year in the UK we spent £594 million on unwanted gifts. The most rewarding gifts are always free and will always be remembered; a helping hand, words of encouragement, support in time of need.

For Further Reflection

Matthew 10:8

God rest ye merry

'Merry Christmas' is a common seasonal
greeting. The Scriptures declare, 'A merry
heart maketh a cheerful countenance.'
So next time you greet someone in this
way you're giving healthy instructions.

For Further Reflection

Proverbs 17:22
Proverbs 15:13

Be considerate

When we express words of appreciation,
we let someone know how valued they are.
Take time to recognise the uniqueness
in someone's life today.

For Further Reflection
Philippians 2:3

You're not alone

For some, Christmas may be a lonely time. It's during these moments that we can be reminded that God is our comforter and true companion in all our times of need.

For Further Reflection

Psalm 23:4

Let God guide you

Jesus, who has the whole world in his hands,
still has room to hold and guide you through
your difficult moments in life.

For Further Reflection

Psalm 31:3

Be the best you can be

'Do all the good you can,
By all the means you can,
In all the ways you can,
At all the times you can!'

John Wesley

_____

For Further Reflection
2 Thessalonians 3:13

Get saved

The name Jesus means 'Saviour', 'Deliverer'. That's exactly what he came to do. That's exactly what he still wants to do.

For Further Reflection

Matthew 1:21

Bring out the child in you!

A recent survey revealed that 61 per cent believed that 'Christmas is mainly for children' ... now that's a good excuse to regress into the world of a child.

For Further Reflection
Matthew 18:3

Spread the Christmas message

There are many seeking for true meaning
in their lives. Christmas is a window of
opportunity to help them fill that void.

For Further Reflection

Romans 5:8

Let Christ in

Christmas is not as much about opening
our presents, as it is about opening
our hearts.

For Further Reflection
Revelation 3:20

The mystery of Christmas

The greatest mystery of all is how God became man, born of a virgin. It's an immaculate phenomenon borne by an immaculate God.

For Further Reflection

Luke 1:31

Let God lead

There may be times when it seems God has pressed the mute button and we can't hear him. In these moments be assured, God is very near and has already worked out the best way for you.

For Further Reflection
Isaiah 59:1

An eternal message

The angels announced it was 'good news of great joy', when Christ was born. It's still good news today and his joy is still freely available to all.

For Further Reflection

Proverbs 25:25

The perfect sacrifice

'The Son of God became a son of man,
in order that the sons of men might
become the sons of God.'

C. S. Lewis

For Further Reflection
James 2:5

All things to all people

'For unto us a child is born, unto us a
son is given ... and his name shall be
called Wonderful Counsellor, Mighty God,
Everlasting Father, Prince of Peace.'

For Further Reflection

Isaiah 9:6

Watch out for God's providence

In times of uncertainty, be reminded that God has already sorted out your circumstances in ways that you cannot see.

For Further Reflection

Jeremiah 33:3

Create your joy

Pure joy may be found in the most unlikely
places ... smiling children in a hospital ward,
relaxing in your broken-down comfortable
settee, warm fireside on a cold day.
Joy is where you find it.

For Further Reflection
John 10:10

Look for God's enablings

No other day will be like today, it brings
its unique store of blessings – they are all
around, you just have to notice them.

For Further Reflection

Deuteronomy 28:1–13

Share your feelings

When your loved one hears you say 'I love you', no amount of gifts can replace their deep-seated feeling of appreciation. If you constantly love someone, constantly tell them.

For Further Reflection
Song of Songs 8:7

Value your loved ones

The sweetest things in life are ones
you cannot buy: the gift of good health,
loyalty of friends and a supportive family.
Don't take any of these for granted.

For Further Reflection

Philippians 4:11

Be faithful in the little things

The best things are still the smallest ones ...
a bunch of flowers, an inspiring card with
meaningful words, a hug of appreciation
or even a word of cheer. The best things
still come in small packages.

For Further Reflection

Luke 19:17

Be true to yourself

The human mind is the most powerful healing force in the world, not matched by any drug. So choose happiness – in doing so you liberate endorphins, the body's own natural happy pill.

For Further Reflection

Isaiah 26:3

Don't neglect yourself

Be your own best friend. Reverse the
golden rule. The kindness you do to
others do also to yourself.

For Further Reflection

Galatians 5:14

You're one of a kind

Remind yourself of your God-given qualities,
those areas where you are gifted and do well
naturally. You are unique; there are things
that only you can do better.

For Further Reflection
2 Timothy 1:6

Gifts money can't buy

The most valuable gifts are priceless ...
compliments, encouragement and a
listening ear.

For Further Reflection
1 Thessalonians 5:11

Look on the bright side of life

Laughter lowers your blood pressure, keeps illness at bay, reduces worry, tones up your nervous system, and makes your face more pleasant to look at. Learn from children ... they do it all the time.

For Further Reflection

Matthew 18:3
Matthew 19:14

Joy comes in the morning

Cry and sigh if you want; tomorrow will
provide many new possibilities.

For Further Reflection

Lamentations 3:22–23

Retreat to advance

We tend to think we can only enjoy the
season in the presence of other people.
Remember silence is golden and solitude is
essential for mental renewal. We should all
find time for a moment to ourselves.

For Further Reflection

Matthew 6:6

See disappointments as God's appointments

Disappointments can come at any time.
Rather than seeing them as misfortunes,
view them as the restraining arm of God
shielding us from a worse fate, rescuing us
from a more dangerous situation.

For Further Reflection
Psalm 34:7

Share special moments

We can fully enjoy something when someone we love enjoys it with us.

For Further Reflection

Ecclesiastes 4:9–12

Recharge

The accumulation of problems tends to
sap our energy and can leave us spent and
discouraged. Take time to recharge; 'staying
power' will come to see you through.

For Further Reflection

Isaiah 40:31

Spread love

We are all one in God's world: and the command to love one another is one of the most important ever given for us to follow.

For Further Reflection

John 15:17

Remember the golden rule

Why is it that we tend to hurt the ones we love the most? It's a paradox which ought not to exist; in hurting one another we hurt ourselves.

For Further Reflection
1 John 3:15

You reap what you sow

'Life is a mirror.
If you frown at it, it frowns back.
If you smile, it returns the greeting.'

Thackeray

For Further Reflection
Romans 12:15

Let God use you

Becoming a channel of God's love is the
best way to display the Christmas message.
Let God's love flow through you to become
a blessing to someone else.

For Further Reflection
Matthew 5:46

The greatest gift of all

'Thanks be to God for his unspeakable gift
– indescribable, inestimable, incomparable,
inexpressible ... precious beyond all words.'

Lois Lebar

For Further Reflection
James 1:17

Develop a big heart

If we think of our heart rather than our
purse as the reservoir of our giving,
we will find it full at all times!

For Further Reflection
Malachi 3:10

Complete the cycle

Christmas began in the heart of God. It is only complete when it reaches our hearts which are then given back to God.

_____

For Further Reflection

Job 11:13–15

Let go

When you have been carrying the burden of
many anxieties, it's time to cast your burden
on the Lord and he will sustain you.

For Further Reflection
Psalm 55:22

You're unique

God's love for you is as though you were
the only person in the universe.

For Further Reflection
Jeremiah 31:3

You're absolutely amazing

Take time to dwell on the amazing thought
that you are absolutely precious in the eyes
of God. You are truly loved, valued and
are one of a kind.

For Further Reflection

Psalm 17:8

Rid yourself of hatred

Bear no malice or evil toward anyone;
such feelings will only backfire. Remember
the message of the angel, 'Peace on earth,
goodwill toward men'.

For Further Reflection

Luke 2:14

Move forward on your knees

When life has brought you to your knees,
stay there and exercise the power of prayer.
You will soon get back up and move
forward again. But keep praying!

For Further Reflection
Matthew 21:22

Think positively

What really takes a toll and wrinkles the
soul are negative emotions like worry, doubt
and despair. What keeps the heart young
is a positive outlook.

For Further Reflection
Mark 9:23

Be at peace

Calmness is the ability to develop a state of
inner assurance and tranquillity when things
are chaotic and haywire on the outside.

For Further Reflection
John 14:27

Return good for evil

When Jesus said, 'Love your enemies', he meant every word of it. We never get rid of an enemy by meeting hate with hate. We get rid of an enemy by getting rid of enmity.

For Further Reflection

Romans 12:21

No pain, no gain

We often cry out, 'Why, oh why, oh why?'
In this world we will get pain without the
reason; in heaven, we will have the reason
without the pain.

For Further Reflection

John 16:33

The power of love

It is the blessed life which began in Bethlehem two thousand years ago which is the personification of eternal love.

For Further Reflection

Jude 21

Let Christ reign

There is a big difference between the observance of Christmas Day and keeping Christmas. One is for a moment, the other is for a lifetime.

For Further Reflection

Psalm 146:10

Count your presents

'Count your many blessings,
name them one by one
and it will surprise you what
the Lord has done.'

For Further Reflection

Jeremiah 17:7

Joy to the world

Somehow not only for Christmas
But all the long year through,
The joy that you give to others
Is the joy that comes back to you.

For Further Reflection

John 15:11

Rest ye merry, gentlemen

Today make time to find half an hour for yourself and relax. Reflect on God's goodness and say a simple prayer of thanks.

For Further Reflection
Mark 6:31

He's got your back!

Whatever challenge you're going through,
stop being afraid. Trust God! He has countless
ways to provide for you, of which you
know nothing.

For Further Reflection
Jeremiah 33:3

Silent night

Jesus says, 'Come unto me, all who labour
and are heavy laden, and I will give you rest.'

For Further Reflection
Matthew 11:28–29

Look beyond disappointments

Let go of the past with its mistakes and
mishaps; your future lies ahead of you
with untapped opportunities. Surge ahead
in confidence, knowing that your past
failures are mere stepping stones to
a better tomorrow.

For Further Reflection
Philippians 3:12–13

Do not covet

To be content with what we have is the
greatest and most secure of riches.

Cicero

For Further Reflection

Hebrews 13:5

High-definition vision

Look at the world through the eyes of a child;
you will see the most amazing sights full of
colour and imagination.

For Further Reflection
Matthew 18:3

Be creative this Christmas

What kindness it is to give friends personal gifts made at home ... jars of chutney or jam, lavender bags for linen, homemade biscuits or half a dozen buns.

For Further Reflection

Ephesians 4:32

Open up to joy

How do you achieve joy? Open your mind to
it, look for it. Joy always comes from within
and then radiates out like a beacon.

Violet Patience

For Further Reflection

Psalm 23:5

New every day

Every day is a special day. There are 86,400 seconds of time in each day to do something worthwhile.

For Further Reflection

Lamentations 3:22–23

Peace, goodwill toward all

There's nothing more satisfying when
you have peace in your home – a place free
from tensions and agitation. As much as
it is possible with you, do your best to
keep the peace.

For Further Reflection

Psalm 122:7–8

God knows the way

'Trust in the Lord with all your heart and
lean not on your own understanding;
in all your ways acknowledge him and
he will make your paths straight.'

For Further Reflection

Proverbs 3:5–6

Value friends

'You can't buy friendship,
It's worth more than gold,
And it's true value increases
As the friendship grows old.'

Phylis Ellison

For Further Reflection

Psalm 18:24

It's worth the wait

'Earth has no sorrow that heaven
cannot heal.'

J. Moore

For Further Reflection
2 Corinthians 4:17

Bridge the gulf

Bridges can be crossed. Christmas is an
opportune time to resolve family feuds,
broken friendships and neighbourly disputes.
Try taking the first step to reconciliation.

For Further Reflection
Matthew 5:24

Angels watching over you

Angels appeared to Mary, the shepherds
and Joseph at the birth of Christ. Be assured
that angels are also on the mission of
watching over you each day.

For Further Reflection

Psalm 34:7

Stay resolute

Christmas can often bring emotions that overwhelm us. Don't let the pressures of the day run you down and spoil your moment.

For Further Reflection
1 Peter 5:7

Get some me time

When everyone is smiling and laughing during this time you may feel the complete opposite; the 'spirit' of Christmas is not there. It's okay, take time for yourself, reflect, meditate and pray. Your rejoicing will come in due time.

For Further Reflection
Psalm 37:24

Love one another

Share words of affirmation with your
loved one; if you mean it, say:
'I love you not only for what you are,
but for who I am when I am with you.'

For Further Reflection
Song of Songs 5:2

Dispel the Christmas blues

After the Christmas festivities we can sometimes feel 'dispirited', with dark grey clouds, long nights and cold spells, but the new year draws nigh ... it's a time for new beginnings.

For Further Reflection
Isaiah 43:19

The battle's not yours

There are times when one's faith is weak as it
is pounded with so many trials. The apostle
Paul says, 'When I am weak, then I am strong.'
Let God fight your battles.

For Further Reflection
2 Corinthians 12:10

Don't stay down

Many of life's obstacles can be seen as
potential opportunities to your next platform.
Don't let them keep you down. Learn from
them, and then move forward.

For Further Reflection
Job 13:15

Think happy thoughts

It is a true realism that you are what you think ... you can control your feelings and bring happiness into your life simply by choosing to do so.

For Further Reflection

Philippians 4:8

Treat yourself

To give your best you must feel your best. To feel your best you need to look after yourself and treat yourself well. This Christmas give yourself a well-deserved treat.

For Further Reflection
Micah 6:8

Put first things first

When you overdo things in the hope of
pleasing others, your work may not always
be fully appreciated. Appreciate yourself for
who you are and others will follow suit.

For Further Reflection
Psalm 125:4

Do yourself a favour

We often put others before ourselves.
Maybe you're a caring person, but there's
no harm in sometimes putting yourself first;
a prerequisite to loving others is to
love yourself.

For Further Reflection
Matthew 19:19

Spoil yourself

Lonely this Christmas? Enjoy your own
company, do something special for yourself
... a massage or spa, or curl up with your
favourite book. Let yourself know that
you're worth a treat.

For Further Reflection
Psalm 62:5

It's possible with God

Faced with a challenging task? You can do all things through Christ who strengthens you.

For Further Reflection

Philippians 4:13

Know your limits

Pushing yourself may tick the next item
off your 'to do' list, but at what expense?
Do yourself a favour and listen to your body!

For Further Reflection

Psalm 46:10

Don't burn out!

It's not work that wears us out, but sadness, anxiety and worry. To God all your concerns are his concerns.

For Further Reflection

1 Peter 5:7

Develop an attitude of gratitude

If you want to be miserable then focus on what others have at the expense at what God's given you. Contentment is not getting what you want; it's enjoying what you already have.

For Further Reflection

Colossians 3:15

Appreciate the moment

You can't change what's happened in the
past, but you can ruin a perfectly good
present by worrying about the future!

For Further Reflection
Matthew 6:25–30

The true Father of Christmas

'If you, then, though you are evil, know how
to give good gifts to your children, how much
more will your Father in heaven give good
things to those who ask him?'

For Further Reflection
Matthew 7:11

Let bygones be bygones

The whole purpose of Christ's coming was
to free us from our sins. As you are freely
forgiven, freely forgive.

For Further Reflection
Matthew 6:14

Enjoy your day

The psalmist says, 'This is the day the Lord has made; let us rejoice and be glad in it.'

For Further Reflection
Psalm 118:24

Believe and receive

God wants only the best for you. His promise
is, 'Whatever you ask for in prayer believe that
you have received it, and it will be yours.'

For Further Reflection
Mark 11:24

You're not alone

We all feel lonely and vulnerable at times,
especially during this time of the year,
but remember, 'God is ... a very present
help in trouble.'

For Further Reflection

Psalm 46:1

Take a break

Sometimes taking a short break will help you get the job done faster. When stress threatens your concentration picture yourself in a relaxing environment, take a deep breath, inhale calm, exhale your anxieties. After you've unwound, go back to your job.

For Further Reflection

Mark 6:31

Appreciate the small things

At the end of the day reflect on what was
the best thing that happened to you; now
take time out to give thanks to God.

For Further Reflection

Deuteronomy 28:6

Don't be a Scrooge

One of the benefits of giving is that it
imparts positive principles of generosity
and thoughtfulness. For this reason it is
better to give than to receive.

For Further Reflection

Luke 6:38

Enjoy quiet moments

The most memorable days may not
necessarily be those where something
exciting or wonderfully spectacular happens,
but those that bring simple pleasures like
relaxing by a crackling fireside watching
the flames dance to and fro.

For Further Reflection
Psalm 96:11–12

Good things lie ahead

We are always at the centre of God's mind.
He says, 'For I know the thoughts that I think
towards you ... thoughts of peace and not
of evil, to give you a future and a hope.'

For Further Reflection

Jeremiah 29:11

Stay calm

Psalm 23 is a calming passage of Scripture
'... he makes me lie down in green pastures.
He leads me beside still waters;
he restores my soul.'

For Further Reflection

Psalm 23

Be positive

We tend to focus on the one negative comment or wrong thing that happens to us in comparison to all the positives that take place in our day. Isn't it time we reversed the tables? Don't let negativism have its stubborn way!

For Further Reflection

Ephesians 5:20

Look up

It never hurts your eyesight to look
on the bright side of life.

For Further Reflection

2 Corinthians 9:11

Recharge this Christmas

Whatever the challenge, trial or difficulty,
his strength will be your strength in
your time of need.

For Further Reflection

Job 16:5

Inspire a generation

Use what you have to enrich the lives of others; your life stories and experiences are invaluable treasures that can inspire.

For Further Reflection
1 Timothy 5:1–4

The joy of church

A survey carried out over 28 years showed
people who attend church regularly enjoy
better health, have lower blood pressure,
less depression and stronger immunity.
Make church attendance more than
just a Christmas affair.

For Further Reflection
Acts 2:42

Spread love

Once in a while we all need to hear the words, 'I think you're wonderful'; start the ball rolling and see how quickly these words return to you.

For Further Reflection
Song of Songs 8:7

Lay down your burdens

The inspired hymn writer Joseph Scriven wrote, 'Oh what peace we often forfeit, Oh what needless pain we bear, all because we do not carry everything to God in prayer.' How true!

For Further Reflection

Philippians 4:6–7

Glory to God in the highest

Worshipping God is an exhilarating
experience. Go ahead, get over your
inhibitions and start by opening your heart,
lifting up your hands and praise God.

For Further Reflection

Psalm 29:2

From hopelessness to hopefulness

When we exercise faith in God, he can take a seemingly bleak future, clouded with hopelessness and turn it into a bright positive outlook. Be assured God's already in your future, working things out for you.

For Further Reflection
Jeremiah 29:11

Believe God

What God thinks of you is more important
than the unkind comments others may make
towards you from time to time.

For Further Reflection

1 Samuel 16:7

Esteem one another

Words of affirmation will always create
an atmosphere in your home conducive
to calm and tranquillity.

For Further Reflection
1 Thessalonians 5:11

Top up your love bank

Relationships are like bank accounts:
they're either in deficit or in surplus.
No deposit ... no return!

For Further Reflection

Hebrews 13:1

You're beautifully designed

Sociologists say our behaviour is determined
by our parents and by our environment.
But when Jesus becomes the Lord of your
life, neither nurture nor nature can prevent
you from becoming the object of beauty
God has designed you to be.

For Further Reflection
2 Corinthians 5:17

God knows best

God knows you better than you know
yourself. Trust your life and future to him,
for he knows the best plan for your life.

For Further Reflection

Proverbs 3:5–6

Be a comforter

If you meet someone today who needs
encouragement, go ahead and give it to
them. More people have died through
broken hearts than swelled heads.

For Further Reflection
1 Thessalonians 4:18

The true confidant

One of Christ's names given on his birth
announcement is 'Wonderful Counsellor'.
We can take all our deepest problems to him
for he offers 100 per cent confidentiality.

For Further Reflection

Matthew 6:6

Major in the minors

It's the little things that reveal the chapters of the heart – the little attentions, small incidences and simple acts of kindness that make up the sum of life's happiness.

For Further Reflection
Luke 16:10

Claim the Christmas promises

The Scriptures contain over three thousand promises for help in time of need. Search the Scriptures – you're bound to find gems of comfort to meet your every need.

For Further Reflection

2 Peter 1:4

The close and personal God

Though God upholds the mighty universe
and ensures the steady course of stars, he still
notices the frown that perplexes and the tear
that flows. He pays close attention to
every detail of our lives.

For Further Reflection

Psalm 34:18

Let God take charge

When you face an impossibility let God deal
with it. He may not necessarily deal with it
your way, but he will bring about the best
possible solution. 'What is impossible
with men is possible with God.'

For Further Reflection

Mark 11:22
Luke 18:27

Remember the Sabbath day

Knowing that work and the stresses of life
can wear us down, God gave us a day of rest.
It's called the Sabbath. One day in the week
God calls us to set aside time from work
to rest and be with him.

For Further Reflection
Genesis 2:1–3

You're a work in progress

The best gift you can give yourself is to accept the special person God made you. Despite your flaws, when God develops your character he works on it throughout your lifetime.

For Further Reflection

Job 23:10

Put God first

Our major goal in life is not just to be happy
or satisfied, but to know God for ourselves.
If we do this we will be more than
happy and satisfied.

For Further Reflection
Matthew 6:33

Take one day at a time

God gives us just enough light to see the next
step and that's all we need. Walk in faith!

For Further Reflection

Psalm 27

Bought with a price

God doesn't love you because you're valuable
– you're valuable because he loves you.

For Further Reflection

Romans 5:8

Start your day right

Begin the day with prayer. Your mind will be refreshed and you will be braced to face life's demands.

For Further Reflection

Psalm 55:17

You're the apple of his eye

Don't say, 'I'm not good enough.' If that's the case then you're God's first mistake and God does not make mistakes.

For Further Reflection

Zechariah 2:8